PROJECT HAPPINESS

273 LITTLE TIPS AND BIG IDEAS FOR FINDING JOY

SOPHIE GOLDING

vie

PROJECT HAPPINESS

Copyright © Summersdale Publishers Ltd, 2017

Research by Agatha Russell.

Summersdale Publishers Ltd
46 West Street
Chichester
West Sussex
PO19 1RP
UK

www.summersdale.com

Printed and bound in Croatia

ISBN: 978-1-84953-972-2

Substantial discounts on bulk quantities of Summersdale books are available to corporations, professional associations and other organisations. For details contact general enquiries: telephone: +44 (0) 1243 771107, fax: +44 (0) 1243 786300 or email: enquiries@summersdale.com.

INTRODUCTION

We often spend a lot of time planning for happy occasions, but actually, life is full of opportunities to experience joy – all we need is to become aware of them and to open ourselves up to the possibilities for happiness offered by everyday life. This book is full of ideas to help you seize those moments of joy and live them to the full.

But seriously for a moment...

Buy yourself the brightest, most beautiful **umbrella** you can find. This will be a reminder to you that there are bright spots on even the greyest of days. Happiness and positivity are, largely, a choice, and we can all make the best out of life if we alter our reactions to situations that we may perceive as negative. Although it may be raining, you can have your own ray of sunshine with a gorgeous brolly.

Dedicate time to **colouring in**. To colour a page allows us to switch our minds off from the stresses of the outside world, and when doing this we focus on the moment. While we follow the patterns and detail, filling the spaces with rich colour, our minds slow down and relax. This means that with a calm brain, free from anxiety we can process situations in a rational way. The more stress-free we feel, the better we can focus on what is important, the happier we can be.

Proverbs are a
garland of ancient
precious jewels to
wear around the
mind and the heart.

Bhutanese proverb

Compliment someone today and mean it, even if that person is a stranger. Often we think nice things and never get around to saying them. Insecurities can make us worry that what we have to say won't be well received or it will sound overeager. The next time something lovely pops into your head, just say it. Perhaps your friend's hair looks great in plaits or they did something thoughtful for you or someone else. A compliment can lift someone else's day, and making someone feel good makes us feel good.

- - - - - - - - -

Do something utterly ridiculous or just plain **silly** every day: wade waist high into the cold sea on a winter's day or make paper planes and throw them around the room. It is important to laugh, to do the unexpected and to challenge ourselves. If we feel sad we are less inclined to take on these surprising activities, so if we try to do at least one hare-brained activity a day then we can bring joy into our daily routine.

Wear a **smile** on your face, even if you don't feel like it. There is scientific thinking behind this suggestion. Happiness can be a preference or an attitude; when you aren't feeling your best ask yourself whether you're caught in a cycle of negativity. When we choose to smile it can instantly lift our mood.

Scientists have found that the small act of smiling releases the 'feel good' neurotransmitters: serotonin, endorphins and dopamine. These not only serve to relax the body, but they can slow down your heart rate and blood pressure too. Endorphins are natural pain relievers and the serotonin released by your smile is a great mood-booster. Flashing an ear to ear grin could even benefit your health and it's contagious too, so you'll be sure to spread your joy far and wide.

Take more **time** for yourself. We can try too hard to attain happiness, thinking it is achieved by being active all the time and so we can neglect self-care. Take the time to indulge in some well deserved 'me time'. Run a candlelit bubble bath or sit down in a quiet room and read the pages of a new novel; do whatever it is that makes *you* happy.

- ➤

Make a **list** of the things that you *think* will make you happy and then write down a list of the things that *have* made you happy. You might be surprised by the disparity. On the first list we often write down objects: when I buy a new car, or when I get that beautiful new house. And on the second list often we write: I met up with old friends, or I walked the dog on the beach. Research has shown that people adapt to physical objects, so the material things you have bought will bring you decreasing amounts of happiness as you adjust to them. It's often the experiences and the people in your life that really make a difference, so endeavour to pursue these sources of happiness over material objects.

Write down a selection of your most blissful **memories**, your best achievements and the most positive traits about yourself; tuck it away into a jacket or purse that you only use rarely. You will most likely forget it's there, but when you rediscover it, the feeling of surprise will only add to the pleasure you feel being reminded of such good times.

- - - - - - - -

Next time you go out for dinner, close your eyes and point to a dish on the menu.

Your meal will be a mystery! Many of us thrive on routine, visiting the same restaurant each time we go out and ordering exactly the same meal every time we are there. It is the fear of the unknown that keeps us in this habit, so by leaving your choice completely up to **chance**, you are training your mind to take risks. If we take risks we grow and if we grow we increase our chances of happiness.

Try a new kind of **tea**. Humans have been relaxing over a cup of delicious tea for thousands of years. And is it any wonder: tea is a wonderful antioxidant, relieves our stresses and tastes great.

An amino acid called theanine, which appears in black or green tea, especially the matcha, gyokuro and anji bai cha varieties, reduces our anxiety levels as it increases the number of neurotransmitters that balance our mood. It also adjusts our serotonin and dopamine levels, which makes us feel happy! Tea drinking has even been said to have similar effects to meditation, stimulating alpha brainwaves associated with deep states of relaxation and enhanced clarity of the mind.

When you are next wandering down the tea and coffee aisle of your local supermarket, branch out and dare to try a whole new flavour. Here are a few types of tea that might take your fancy and possess the properties to perk up your mood: ginger tea is great to bring you back to life on a sleepy day, hibiscus tea reduces blood pressure and peppermint tea is a natural stimulant and mood-booster. Tea really is the closest thing to buying happiness.

Always believe that you have a **purpose**. To be truly happy, humans like to value themselves and feel that they contribute to society. Your purpose doesn't have to be a career, it should be more like a message that you carry with you and give out during your life. It could be to 'empower women to realise their worth and potential', 'to help those that are in need' or 'to always be as kind as possible'. Think of what it is that's important to you, and see how you can contribute to this cause. It can be as simple as dedicating a little money or time a month.

-->

Tell someone you **love** them and mean it. 'I love you' is one of the most important things you can say, although we often forget to do it, assuming our loved ones already know. Remember the phrase's importance and the impact it can have on you and the person you are saying it to. 'I love you' provides you both with a moment to focus on each other.

> NATURE DOES NOT HURRY, YET EVERYTHING IS ACCOMPLISHED.
>
> Lao Tzu

Remember to **slow down**. Many of us go about our daily lives at 100 mph and this can induce stress. Stress is often the thing that makes us feel most unhappy; it raises our heart rate, our blood pressure and cortisol levels – the stress hormone in the body. While we cannot always avoid stress, we can find ways to deal with it effectively. One way is to remember that taking life at a slightly slower pace can help us become happier people; we are more able to process events and emotions when we have time and aren't rushing to our next 'must do'.

Do one **kind thing** for someone else. Lend someone a book they've always wanted to read, help them decorate their home, cook them their favourite food, or do whatever else it is that you think would help them out. Kindness is contagious, so in theory if we are all more generous with each other, others will be generous with us too. Happy endorphins are released when we give. Your time is precious, so aim for an act of kindness every day but don't feel pressured by a schedule; you'll find it will occur more often as it gets folded into your lifestyle.

Spend a day **de-cluttering** your home. Having too much unnecessary stuff can be the source of unhappiness and stress, and clutter-free surfaces make your home feel simple, tranquil and relaxing. Be ruthless with the things you really don't need or especially don't want and donate them to a charity. You could even have a car boot sale with some of your unwanted possessions. Not only do you make your house feel calmer and cleaner, but you give the things you don't want to a better home.

Get the rollers and paintbrushes out and **redecorate** at least one room in your home this month. A fresh new colour can transform your living space. Homes are our sanctuaries so it is important that we keep them feeling cosy and welcoming.

Take your time and find joy in choosing the new look, even making collages of the look you really want. You can be creative with your redesign: paint the floorboards, invest in a beautiful new rug, think of new places for furniture or make space for some house plants. With their oxygenating leaves, plants are especially good additions to your home, helping to lower anxiety and blood pressure. Keep the ideas of preserving space and de-cluttering in mind; too many new additions to the room and you may feel enclosed and hemmed in. When you are done, light a scented candle and relax in your lovely reimagined space.

Appreciate the **days off** that you have. Weekends and days that we have to ourselves are said to be when we are at our happiest. Scientists have found that regardless of our career choice, moods are boosted at the weekends. Remember to plan your time and utilise it well, and attempt to balance what must be done with what you want to do.

Use positive **affirmations** to guide your subconscious. Research has found that we should use phrases that are tailored to our individual personalities, as these will be far more effective than generic statements in changing and improving our state of mind and mood. When creating a positive affirmation consider your needs and what aspect of yourself you would like bolstered. For example 'I take pleasure in my solitude' might work for some, or 'I love and approve of myself' would be preferable to others.

He who lives in harmony with himself lives in harmony with the universe.

Marcus Aurelius

Aim to surround yourself with **positive people**. Outside influences are often out of our control, but when we have the chance we choose to spend time with positive people. True friends uplift each other and want to make each other feel good, even in a negative situation. Keep this in mind when choosing your friends, and stick with people who want the best for you. If your friends are positive and loving they will have a healthy effect on your mood.

Consume **positive propaganda** – however crazy that may sound. Read uplifting material, blogs or books; watch and listen to positive vloggers or podcasts. Open yourself up to a world of positivity and happiness by accessing the wealth of information out there. It is important to keep up with the world's events but the news is undoubtedly weighted to the negative. Counteract the stream of sad and serious news with uplifting and light-hearted material and you'll soon realise the world is as full of the good as the bad.

Strive to **meditate** for 5–10 minutes every day. Recent studies have shown us that we can elevate our happiness levels through regular meditative practice. Meditation is one of those exercises that we can use to gather our thoughts, focus on what's important, and ultimately lessen the stresses that can bring us down. It increases the amount of grey matter in the part of the brain that is related to happiness.

Meditation is an effective method of achieving relaxation but for the unpractised, it is an unfamiliar state of being. Don't put yourself under pressure if at first you are easily distracted during your meditation, as this is very common. If unwanted thoughts enter your head, don't try to suppress them, as this is likely to distract you even more. Be in a state of acceptance rather than rejection and simply acknowledge that they are there. You'll find that the practice of acknowledging thoughts and feelings, but not acting on them, will not only improve your meditative ability but also be a useful life skill.

Pamper yourself by getting a massage or visiting a health spa and watch your worries float away in the steam room, dissolving in the eucalyptus haze. Feeling relaxed is an essential aspect of feeling happy. Going to a place dedicated to relaxation is a great way to break the stress cycle and allow yourself to stop worrying. (Your smartphone won't work in the steam room, after all!) Gift yourself the chance to simply take a moment, reflect and feel anew.

- - - - - - - - -

The way we look is not everything, but when we wear **clothes** that make us feel attractive it can give our confidence a boost. Dress up in your best outfit, spend time doing your make-up or styling your hair, and allow yourself to feel great about your appearance. You deserve to feel good about your looks and to show yourself off.

Happiness is when
what you think,
what you say,
and what you do
are in harmony.

Mahatma Gandhi

Sing a song out loud so that everyone can hear, even if you don't think of yourself as a gifted singer. While we may not all be vocalists with star potential, partaking in a little spontaneous karaoke can release our inhibitions. Start with the old favourite – singing in the shower. Not only will you have an audience of just one, everyone's voice sounds better in the shower too, so you'll get a little boost of confidence upon hearing yourself.

Build castles in the sand. It is common for us to think of ourselves at the centre of the universe, but it is important to remind ourselves that we are equal to everything else on our beautiful planet. Time passes and no matter what we do or what we try to leave behind, change is always with us. Make patterns and castles in the sand and watch as they crumble under the tide. It is important that we accept change and learn to celebrate it.

Try a **yoga laughter** class. Hasyayoga is a practice that involves voluntary laughter, although when you give it a go you will quickly realise that forced laughter turns into the genuine kind. Developed by physician Madan Kataria, laughter yoga combines laughing and additional breathing techniques, which encourage more oxygen into the body and brain. Studies have shown that laughter directly lowers stress levels and in turn improves the immune system and so just like smiling, within minutes, laughter can transform your mood to cheerful. To giggle with others provides a positive energy too, which helps us to improve relationships and connect. So, if you laugh more you will attract many new friends and reinforce relationships with the people you already know.

Plant a tree and give yourself a vital lesson in patience. Watch it grow, nurturing it and helping it in its journey. Instant gratification often seems like a must nowadays: our technology allows us instantaneous results, the service at a restaurant must be quick and even travelling long distances doesn't take long. Developing patience allows us to gain a sense of perspective on time. You'll find a surprising satisfaction in helping something young grow to its full potential, learning that magnificent outcomes take time, perseverance and a little faith.

- - - - - - - -

Learn to speak a new **language**. It could be something more familiar like French or Spanish, or a more distant language such as Russian or Chinese. Learning is an excellent way of stimulating our brains. Studies have shown that through learning to speak another language we engage with other cultures, giving us a broader emotional perspective that can help us to stay happy, healthy and balanced.

> True happiness is not attained through self-gratification, but through fidelity to a worthy purpose.
>
> Helen Keller

Go out and join a **group activity**. It could be playing tennis or golf, partaking in a quick game of ping pong or perfecting your brush strokes in an art class. Not only will you be exercising your brain but you'll be opening yourself up to new connections and relationships. You'll enjoy all the best things in life: new experiences, learning and human interaction.

Set yourself a new challenge. A limitation is something that we set for ourselves, either through fear or a lack of faith in our abilities. Your challenge could be to climb the dizzying heights of a mountain and look down upon the world from cold peaks; it could be initiating conversation with a stranger. Anything that pushes past those limitations we often make for ourselves would work. Set your sights on something that feels out of your reach and do it.

- ▶

Pick a letter of the alphabet and centre your day's activities on that letter. If your letter was 'B' you could have bagels for lunch, balance on every wall you walk past or boogie down to some sweet tunes. These little acts of randomness will lift an ordinary day into a day of discovery.

Challenge yourself and for one whole day strive to say **yes** to everything asked of you. Make this a one-day challenge to avoid putting too much on your plate at first; you'll be amazed at the unexpected places it leads you to. Choose a time when you do not have lots of stressors, in order to allow for the extra mental or time capacity that may be needed when taking on things that are outside the norm.

By saying yes to more we may be helping others or going outside our comfort zones into more sociable situations. By avoiding circumstances that may have risks of sadness such as a new relationship or friendship, we could be avoiding and missing out on chances to be happy. The emotions we feel are temporary and with every thought of sadness comes happiness, with jealousy comes gratitude and so on. So when we accept that sadness is just a natural emotion that passes like any other, we then have the faith and the confidence to say yes to more.

When chaos and pandemonium reigns, firmly wedge in some ear plugs and enjoy your **inner peace**. It is said that silence is where happiness begins; it is the place beneath our inner dialogue that holds our ability to love, to wonder, to have compassion, to burst with new ideas. Take time to sink far below the crashing waves and go into the quiet. When we emerge we are calmer, clearer beings.

- - - - - - - - -

Look across to views of other **cultures** on happiness. Taking a step back and listening to others can give us a wider opinion, so look to other ways of life and their techniques for dealing with ups and downs. Bhutan, in the Eastern Himalayas, takes an out of the ordinary attitude to happiness; His Majesty, King Wangchuck, measures the country's success on Gross National Happiness, and values this over Gross National Product.

In the midst of
movement and
chaos, keep stillness
inside of you.

Deepak Chopra

Write down all of your hopes and desires and put them up in a room in your house so that you can see them. Visualising your greatest goals can make them feel tangible, and if those goals are turned into aspirations which we can see happening, we are more inclined to be able to achieve them. Don't keep them tucked away in the depths of your mind; instead have them on show for you to see and be inspired by every day.

Be thankful for the things around you. Showing gratitude is one way of being more positive about your life and the things that are in it. Be thankful for the body that you have, and all that you are capable of. Be grateful for the triumphs you have already achieved in your lifetime. Negativity is easier for our brains to process than positivity is, so it is important to remind ourselves of the most important things, the positives.

Embrace your **inner child**. Children have a marvellous way of being astonished by the simplest of events; these events seem to pass adults by as their responsible lives take hold. Take time to appreciate Mother Nature, whether by valuing the colours in the morning sky on the way in to work, or noticing how the buds on the flowers are formed so delicately when you sit in the garden or walk through the park.

Exercising our innate sense of curiosity means that we are truly involved and actively interested in something – it helps to build our wonder and intrigue. With a little practice we can transform tasks that would otherwise be mundane routines, into small joyful events. Being inclined towards curiosity makes us more likely to be open to a new challenge or event, so that we gain more from unfamiliar experiences. Life is satisfying when you are interested in living it, so use your innate sense of curiosity to your advantage.

Lie down in the snow, stretch out your arms way above your head and bring them to your sides to make snow angels. If you haven't got snow, go out into the sunshine and lie down in the spiky tufts of grass and make grass angels; you won't be able to see them but you'll be able to feel their outline around you. We often lose touch with nature in modern society and, with that, we leave behind an important natural source of happiness.

- ➤

Go outside and bask in the sunlight. With the changeable weather, venturing outside might be something that we don't often do, but it is important on a dry day to take advantage of it. Most of our vitamin D is produced from direct sunlight and sunlight also helps our bodies to make serotonin, the 'happy hormone'. Throughout the winter months, fewer daylight hours can make us feel slightly more tired as our brains produce melatonin, the 'sleep hormone'. So short bursts of sunlight, 10–15 minutes, can provide us with a valuable boost to our mood and our health.

THE MOMENTS OF HAPPINESS

WE ENJOY TAKE US BY SURPRISE.

IT IS NOT THAT WE SEIZE THEM,

BUT THAT THEY SEIZE US.

Ashley Montagu

Boost your intake of **vitamin B**. Vitamin B is particularly important in the control of tryptophan, the amino acid key in the production of serotonin. Low moods can often come from low levels of tryptophan and therefore low serotonin levels. Vitamins B1, B3, B5, B6, B9 and B12 are all found in a healthy and balanced diet, in particular spinach, broccoli, avocado, egg, poultry and liver. Fortified cereals and alternative milk products are also a great source too. Vitamin B helps to release energy in carbohydrates, proteins and fats, so for that extra boost of happy energy, top up on vitamin B.

- →

Cut out the sweet stuff. When low moods strike, it is particularly tempting to dip into a bag of sweets or to indulge in a sticky cake, but resist: these sweet treats are not mood-boosters for long. It is our innate fight or flight response that makes us reach for sugary foods, as they give us an instant quick-release of energy. However, the sharp rise in the energy we gain from sugar is followed by a swift fall, and in the long run it can make us feel more depressed. So to satisfy your sweet tooth, try eating foods that are naturally sweet, such as coconut, fresh fruit and berries, nuts, carrots and sweet potatoes.

Join the **gym** with a good friend or family member and make special dates to go there together on a regular basis. If the gym doesn't appeal, play tennis, cycle or go jogging together. Being fit and healthy, in whatever way you choose, is important in being happy.

Exercise makes us feel more confident about ourselves and our body. It gives us a sense of purpose and accomplishment. These are great factors in improving our mood, however there's even more to it than that. When we begin to exercise, our brain perceives this as a moment of stress. As the brain prepares for a fight or flight response it protects itself by releasing BDNF (Brain-Derived Neurotrophic Factor). This protein protects and repairs memory function and almost acts like a reset button. This can explain why we can feel clearer headed and calmer after exercise.

Chemicals called endorphins are also released by the brain. The endorphins fight stress and can minimise pain when exercising, and even induce feelings of euphoria in many people. With just 20 minutes of exercise your mood can be boosted for 12 hours.

Plunge into the water and **swim**. Swimming can be a great way to centre ourselves after a busy day at work, not to mention the fact that it is a full-body workout. It is one of the most effective forms of exercise, toning many parts of the body simultaneously. As the water surrounds you, concentrate on the calming way it swishes through your fingers and toes. Focus on your breathing with each stroke you take and allow yourself to reach a tranquil state as you propel yourself smoothly through the water.

- - - - - - - - -

Cut down on the amount of alcohol you drink. Many of us feel that there is nothing better than a cool glass of beer or wine after work, but although alcohol does have an instantly pleasant effect on our mood, research shows that this is only a temporary happiness. Alcohol is a depressant, and feelings of anxiety and stress can remain after the more enjoyable effects wear off. Reduce the amount of drinking you do as much as possible to feel more balanced and positive.

Eat **good fats**; they do exist, and we actually rely upon them for healthy brain function. Research suggests that people who cut out all fats in their diet, as they strive for good health, can feel stressed, anxious and depressed. Baked goods, snacks and fried food contain trans fats, which are bad for us, and so we should minimise our intake of these. At the same time, we should enjoy plenty of polyunsaturated fats, found in walnuts, sesame, peanuts, oily fish, olive oil and sunflower seeds, and increase our intake of monounsaturated fats by eating nuts, olives and avocados.

Eat your **five a day**. Five portions of fruit and vegetables a day are recommended, but if you manage more than this, your body will thank you. Fruit and vegetables containing vitamins B and C are good for your brain function, which will help you to feel calm and happy. Asparagus, green leafy vegetables, beetroot, romaine lettuce, turnip and lentils are rich in B vitamins, and you'll find vitamin C in yellow bell peppers, broccoli, berries, citrus fruit, kiwi fruit, tomatoes, peas, papayas and guava.

A **balanced diet** is key to feeling happier. Selecting the right food can be daunting when so much of the available information on nutrition is conflicting. The NHS Choices website suggests using the traffic light information system on food packaging, as a good 'beginners' way to judge whether a food will be a healthy or unhealthy choice. The colours help you tell at a glance whether a food is high in something you've already had a lot of that day, such as salt or sugar, and the more precise percentages help you assess where you are with your recommended daily allowances.

Grow your own fruit, vegetables or flowers, whether it's herbs on the window sill, tomato plants on the patio or a whole bed of dahlias.

When you are out watering the flowers or picking ripe fruit listen to the birdsong, feel the breeze on your face and enjoy the sun's warm rays on your skin. As well as absorbing vitamin D from sunlight there are a few other things that gardening can do to help with our happiness. It has been said that smelling the roses and uprooting weeds from the ground can increase brain activity, lower blood pressure and produce feelings of cheerfulness. Even the dirt under fingernails can help: friendly soil bacteria called *Mycobacterium vaccae* can help to ease symptoms of depression.

Growing our own food makes us more aware of how fruit and vegetables come to be. From relying upon warmer weather to bring on quick growth and ripe fruit, to slugs and rabbits nibbling away at growing leaves, gardening can make us appreciate where our food has come from and its constant availability. Stopping to think about our food allows us to stop and appreciate how lucky we are.

Drink **more water**. Staying hydrated prevents headaches and keeps your head feeling fresh and clear. According to studies even mild dehydration can cause an alteration in energy and mood, affecting memory, concentration and perception, and increasing anxiety and fatigue. The European Food Safety Authority suggests drinking 2 litres of water per day for men and 1.6 litres for women. However these levels can change due to heat, exercise and other factors. Drinking little and often is really the key.

- - - - - - - - -

Make sure that you are getting enough **sleep**. Sleep is how our bodies recharge themselves, and getting the right amount has an important positive effect on us. Improving our sleep will help us to feel happier and think clearly. The average adult needs around 7–9 hours sleep a night, but every person differs between those amounts. Listen to the way your body feels according to how much sleep you are getting, until you find the right balance.

Tension is who you think you should be, relaxation is who you are.

Chinese proverb

Writing a **journal**, even if it's only one sentence a day, can help us to keep happy memories vivid, and allows us to reflect back over the day and find something enjoyable about it… even if we originally perceived it to be a bad day. Appreciating the good things about our day helps us to feel happy about it. We all tend to enjoy rediscovering memories, small or significant, and when you read back through your journal after a few months of daily jotting, you're likely to experience a great sense of joy.

It is known too that our brains are designed for survival. In the past our lives were often under threat, and so our brains are inclined to processing negative information over positive. It may have kept us alive years ago but it isn't so useful nowadays. By keeping a one sentence journal we are reminding ourselves of the positives that our brains do not process as well.

Take up **rambling**. Walking is a brilliant way to balance our mood: we are outdoors stretching our legs amongst nature, and just as when we're at the gym, serotonin, the 'happy hormone', is released. Walking is such a simple form of exercise that it can easily be fitted in around our daily routine. You could park further away from work, go for a walk at lunch time or take the dog for a walk before and after work. Make walking, in whatever form, a habit and your body will thank you for it.

◄ –

Cycle into work for a week. Exercise is a dependable mood-booster and even 10 minutes of cycling can improve your outlook and harness a little more positivity. Cycling to work is the perfect way to fit exercise into your daily routine, and cycling on a regular basis strengthens not only your body but your mind too.

Happiness is not a
station you arrive
at, but a manner
of travelling.

Margaret Lee Runbeck

Find **positives** within the negatives. We all experience difficult situations from time to time but, by shifting our perspective, we can deal with them in a better light. Looking for positives may be difficult to do, but if you persevere your hard work will pay off. For example, if a relationship has ended, try to find a way of thinking to which allows you to be happy that a new stage of your life is beginning, with uncountable unknown possibilities in store. A shift in your perspective can be healing.

Live for today. Many of us spend our time thinking of the past or the future, neglecting to really live in the now. **Zazen**, which is Japanese for 'sitting meditation', sets out to centre the body and the mind. Sit with your legs crossed and your back straight, and concentrate on breathing deeply. By focusing your mind on breathing, your thoughts are brought right back into the present, and can help to give you a new way of seeing the world.

Start your day with a '**smiling meditation**'. Close your eyes and take in deep, relaxing breaths. Imagine that you are inhaling peace and exhaling calm.

Feel the breaths flooding into every part of your body. Perhaps you will see them as washes of colour or long ribbons of glitter.

Exhale your worries and stresses, release any tensions you may have, and feel the weight of your body relax around you.

When you feel ready, smile. It can be just a small smile. Sit there quietly for a while smiling.

Imagine now that your smile is travelling up through your cheeks. Visualise that your nose is smiling and even though they are closed, your eyes are smiling too.

Your eyelashes are smiling and so are your ears; they are warm with delight. Your forehead is smiling and even your hair is radiating a glowing grin.

The smiles move down into your neck and chest, your heart is beaming bright. Soon every single part of you is grinning, all the bones in your toes, all the cells racing through your body.

Illuminate your home. In India, the Hindu celebration of Diwali, Festival of Lights, is an opportunity to welcome peace into your life and into your spirit; it is a chance to start afresh. During the festival, people cleanse their homes and await the arrival of Lakshmi Goddess of Good Fortune, Ganesha the Remover of Obstacles and Hanuman Lord of Auspicious Beginnings. Our environments have a great influence on who we are and the way we feel, so take a little from Diwali, cleanse your home and light it up with glittering candles.

- - - - - - - - -

Go to an **art gallery** and spend time admiring the artwork. Going to observe art and sculpture is a creative way of appreciating someone else's interpretation or reading of the world, or a particular time or situation. Doing this can help you to gain some perspective upon your own life and see it from a new perspective. Inspiring and refreshing, artwork can allow our minds to get lost in thought.

> Art enables us to find ourselves and lose ourselves at the same time.

Thomas Merton

Paint a picture. Even if you aren't a skilled artist, painting is therapeutic and can bring great happiness. Greater creativity can bring greater contentment, and it has even been found that those who practise art regularly are better at solving problems. Let the brush guide you around the canvas or page, and take pleasure watching the colours run into each other. Paint a scene or an abstract emotion and see where the creativity takes you.

Spring-clean your aura. We need to remind ourselves that we can start anew whenever we feel like it. Sometimes this is the best way to improve our mood, by starting afresh with a clean slate. Consider your current thoughts and emotions: is there anything negative that you are holding on to unnecessarily? Petty annoyances such as being cut up while driving, or a shop sold out of your favourite food can frustrate at the time but shouldn't be on your mind hours later. Make a conscious decision to let those concerns go.

Be more mindful. Mindfulness is a Buddhist technique that aims to make you fully aware of your environment, your thoughts and your actions while you experience them. If you train the mind to notice the details that are happening in the present, you can fully experience your life and enjoy it as it happens. This will help you avoid the feeling of 'drifting' and assist in identifying what you would like to change, and what truly makes you happy.

When you are next surrounded by others in a social situation try to be more mindful in your **interactions**. Often during exchanges with others we can interpret behaviours wrongly and this can cause conflict, bring down our mood, and cause stress to ourselves and others.

Listen more deeply and truly take in the body language of the person you're speaking with. We are all capable of engaging with others in a more meaningful way and if we take the time to notice and sense behaviours around us, it will improve our social connections with others.

We can also be more mindful in our own behaviours. Take into consideration what you want to say and take the time to choose the best possible way to express it. Pay attention to your facial expressions and hand gestures. By learning to communicate better, we can become happier, and the people around us will feel the benefit too.

We know that there are different factors influencing our happiness levels. Some are determined genetically, which we can't do much about; some stem from past events, and although we can come to terms with these and move forwards, the effects will be part of our happiness make-up, and it's important to understand this to be truly contented; but it may help to realise that at least 40 per cent of our happiness is completely in **our control** in the here and now. We have the power to make that 40 per cent the best it can be, and to live our most joyful lives.

- - - - - - - - -

Cook a meal and invite your family to come and **share** it with you. Spending time with our families helps us to understand our context and gives us a sense of belonging. When we leave home it is easy to get caught up in our own personal commitments and spend much less time around relatives. Making set occasions in our diaries to see our families can bring us great happiness, and help us to greater understand who we are.

follow your
own star.

Dante

Remind yourself that you don't need to compare yourself to other people. Every single person on the planet is completely and utterly different, and each personality has totally unique traits. We often forget to give ourselves credit for our own qualities and achievements, and it is easy to look to others and make unfair comparisons. By accepting ourselves for exactly who we are and knowing that we don't need to be the same, we can learn to appreciate others and ourselves equally.

- -

Go to Holi festival. The Hindu Festival of Colour rejoices in individuality, by taking people away from the throes of daily life and helps them to let loose and release stressful inhibitions. Merrymakers douse each other with water and fistfuls of vibrant colour to celebrate the beginning of spring. Many major cities host their own Holi festival celebrations and there are even secular activities, such as 'colour runs' where runners are splashed with paint, inspired by the festival.

Remember to **hug** those you love, whenever the moment is right. There are many amazing benefits to a cuddle that not only improve our health, but make us happier people too.

The 'love hormone' known as oxytocin increases when we hug and touch each other. The higher our levels of oxytocin, the better equipped we are to deal with life's stresses. Hugging is also known to lower the stress hormone, cortisol, and there's even more to it than that. Our skin is covered in tiny, egg shaped pressure centres that when touched send a signal to the brain. So a 20-second hug, accompanied by 10 minutes of hand holding reduces the physical effects of stress, lowering our blood pressure and reducing our heart rate. When we hug someone it increases our social connections and our sense of belonging so improving the relationships we have with the people in our lives. We must never underestimate the power of the hug.

Practise **compassion** in your daily life; you can start by trying to change your mindset, such as judging people by their intentions rather than their actions. If you are seeking a practical way to invite compassion into your life, consider volunteering for a charity or not-for-profit organisation. This may help you feel that you are having a positive effect on your community, and help you cultivate empathy and affection for those around you.

- - - - - - - -

Learn to say **no**. Saying no can be seen as a negative thing but is sometimes the healthiest, wisest choice for you and those around you. We can commit to too many events or too much of a workload out of fear of disappointing others. The feeling of being under pressure isn't healthy for you, and being unable to deliver on your promises because you are overstretched isn't helpful to those around you. Assessing whether you have the time or resources to assist with a task and reporting back honestly, is the best choice for everyone.

Be content
with what
you have; rejoice in
the way things are.
When you realise
there is nothing
lacking, the world
belongs to you.

Lao Tzu

Take the afternoon off and indulge yourself. This might be watching feel-good rom-coms, spoiling yourself with delicious cake, or opening a bottle of bubbly you have been saving for a special occasion. It is sometimes good to side-line duty and obligation and enjoy guilt-free leisure and pleasure. Small pleasures can often give us a dose of much needed happiness.

Get up early and go outside to photograph the sunrise. Most people miss the sunrise, especially in summer, as they are asleep when it takes place. Set your alarm, go to bed early and, on rising, grab your camera and find an idyllic spot to appreciate the miracle of the sun starting the day. This will make you feel accomplished, having experienced beauty with the whole day still to come.

Dare yourself to **disconnect** from social media for one whole day. Smartphones and tablets now allow us to access the web and social media sites at whatever time of the day we want. While the internet can impact our life positively, by providing quick answers to our questions and connecting us with people all over the world, it can also have some quite negative effects on our well-being.

Social media has made it much easier to compare our lives to other people's. However, you will only be seeing the very best events; you will not be seeing their average days, their not-so-good days or even their dull days. It isn't helpful to compare your everyday activities to someone else's highlights reel.

By separating yourself from the internet for one whole day, you can free yourself from these comparisons. Simply live your life for the day, concentrate on your actions instead of checking your devices and focus on your own happiness instead of being a spectator to someone else's. You may find your day to be a peaceful one.

Spend an afternoon outside truly engrossed in a **book** that you have been meaning to read for ages. Turn off electronic devices, clear your schedule and simply enjoy fresh air and the words in front of your eyes. Passing the hours focused on one activity is a peaceful and uncluttered way to invite joy into your life.

- - - - - - - - -

Pick some sloes and make **sloe gin**. Producing something yourself rather than purchasing it ready-made can be rewarding. Immerse yourself in a creative process – happiness can come from both tangible results and sharing those with family and friends. Go outside and pick 450 g of sloes, then bring them home. Prick the skins and put them in a large sterilised jar. Add 225 g of caster sugar and 1 litre of gin. Seal tightly and shake. Leave in a cool dark cupboard and shake every other day for a week. Then shake once a week for at least two months.

DOING WHAT YOU LIKE IS
FREEDOM. LIKING WHAT YOU
DO IS HAPPINESS.

Frank Tyger

Give yourself a **project** to sink your teeth
into. Get involved in a new hobby or activity
and make a positive change in your life.
Projects or hobbies can give us a focus
and they can alter our views on life for the
better. Whether it be joining a yoga class or
book club, running or knitting with friends
or joining a gardening club, we can gain joy
from being around others that have a similar
interest. Being involved can take our mind
off our problems and open it to happiness.

Listen to more music. Give your life a soundtrack and make more time for melody. The human brain is hardwired to react emotionally to and interpret music. Studies show that the body reacts physically to the mood of music we are listening to. Music with a major tone and faster tempo has been found to quicken breathing, a sign of happiness. Music has even been seen to improve happiness in patients after surgery, lower stress in pregnant women and decrease blood pressure in cardiac patients.

Visit meaningful places that have featured highly in your memory. The familiar sights, smells and sounds can soothe you and bring to mind those happy memories. When you feel shaken, the familiar can be comforting, help you feel centred and give you a sense of home. Although it is important to not always be living in the past, acknowledging your roots can be healthy.

A study has suggested that we gain more pleasure from spending money on **experiences** than on material objects. People tend to adapt to an object, no matter what it is, meaning that the things we buy will bring us decreasing amounts of happiness as time goes on. Lasting happiness, however, is better found in one-off experiences that we can look back upon with increasing amounts of joy. Humans never get bored of memories, so the more we make the more we have to feel happy about.

One big experience could be to pack your bags and **travel**. Travelling to a new place can open our minds to different cultures and ways of life, while providing us with an unforgettable experience. Planning a trip can also be an exciting experience, as we immerse ourselves in the details, researching and anticipating our upcoming journey. It can make our everyday lives more enjoyable when we know that something great is definitely coming our way.

Teach yourself to take life **less seriously**. It might not feel fantastic to hear 'lighten up' immediately after the sting of an ill-judged joke or frustration, but after some time has passed, reflect on how carrying negative feelings about it affected you. Being brought down by small negatives is simply not worth our time, and laughing or smiling in the face of negativity can physically change our mood: it triggers the release of happy hormones.

- - - - - - - - -

Tend to a **bonsai tree**. These miniature trees are symbols of meditation, harmony, peace, balance; an ordering of thoughts and all that is good about the world. This art form developed from Chinese horticulture, and was then influenced by Japanese Zen Buddhism. The act of mindfully tending to and nurturing your tree can create an oasis of calm in your daily routine.

IN OUR DAILY LIVES, WE MUST SEE
THAT IT IS NOT HAPPINESS
THAT MAKES US GRATEFUL,
BUT THE GRATEFULNESS
THAT MAKES US HAPPY.

Albert Clarke

Don't be held back by things that scare you. By facing up to fears we confront them head on, eliminating some of the unknown that exaggerates them. Whether it's holding a tarantula to overcome your fear of spiders, or talking to a stranger to challenge your social anxieties, staring right into the eyes of fear can be very rewarding.

Break out of your own universe. Many of us find ourselves completely consumed by our own worlds, whether it is focusing on work or paying too much attention to our gadgets. Notice if you are in a rut and endeavour to change your routine. Every evening, strive to take a walk through your neighbourhood or town and share time with others; even meeting up with friends in sociable places can help to remind us that we are part of something bigger.

Studies say there are five steps that we can all take to improving the well-being of our minds: connecting with others, getting active, learning new skills, giving to others and taking notice of the world around us. Cooking is an excellent way to employ some of these steps.

Dedicate a regular night to **cooking with friends**. You could try a Mexican evening and make your own guacamole, or put together some of your favourite recipes.

Cooking is a fantastic way to wind down after a hectic day. It is a nourishing act that centres the mind and allows you to slow down and focus your thoughts. We can often think of cooking as a chore, so having a special evening with friends and loved ones, cooking new, exciting or much loved recipes can make it a little more fun. Not only does the act of cooking have a therapeutic effect on the mind, but this event will bring you and your friends together.

Try t'ai chi. This martial art was developed in thirteenth-century China; today it is used as an exercise, to develop deep breathing techniques and relaxation. It focuses on balancing energy flow through the body, ridding it of blockages. It also promotes the balance of yin and yang. Unlike other sports, t'ai chi uses circular movements that relax the muscles, no motion is forced and joints are not fully extended nor bent. T'ai chi will help you to balance your inner energies and become happier.

Have a little more faith. Although we all like to have control over our lives and the things that we do, there is much that is completely out of our control. Faith, in whatever form we see it, allows us to take all of our worries about uncontrollable variables, and set them apart from ourselves, accepting things the way they are. Faith can be praying to a god, but in other forms, it can be the faith to get on a plane or to take a risk of any kind. Try to let go of the things that you know you cannot control, and concentrate on the aspects you can control.

forgiveness does
not change the
past, but it does
enlarge the future.

Paul Boese

Put your mental well-being before your financial success. It goes without saying that financial stability takes away worry and stress, however, it is often the case that we dedicate our lives to striving for more and more financial success so that we can buy flash cars, tropical getaways, the latest gadgets, opulent houses. Global economic growth has been seen to rise sharply over the past few decades; however well-being has not risen with it. Make sure you don't neglect your well-being for financial ventures.

Our words are powerful and we must never underestimate the impact that they can have on people. Words uttered in haste can often leave a mark on our conscience. The next time that you feel your emotions rising in a moment of dispute, gaze up to the sky, take a deep breath and feel the world's immensity, imagining all the people who live under that vast sky. If now you decide to speak, speak slowly and with carefully chosen words that express your meaning well.

Resolve to take a **photo** every day of the year and create an album to look back on. Whether film cameras or smartphones and tablets are more your thing, photographs in all forms are a great source of happiness for us.

They can act as reminders of fond moments from the past, as channels for creativity or even as visual diaries to record the things that are so precious, yet easily get lost in the many daily events of life. When we recall happy memories, they increase our happiness in the present.

Scientists have also found that those who take photos on a regular basis are more engaged with and immersed in the life experience than those who do not photograph it. This is because those people taking photographs are picking out details in their view and focusing on them: if you are more absorbed in a life event you are more likely to be enjoying it. Taking pictures and looking at them can be a brilliant exercise in improving our happiness levels.

Make **amusing videos** with you and your friends. Whether you are playing a starring role or you are the principal camera operator, video memories are precious, and fun to create. Much like photos, they allow you to revisit fond and treasured memories and they are also a slightly different way to interact with our experiences. For the best memories, video situations where everyone is feeling at ease and completely natural.

— — — — — — — —

Wear the most **colourful outfit** you can find. Scientists have found that brighter colours fill us with a sense of happiness. Colour affects us throughout life, even if we aren't always aware of it. Pink is the colour of adoration and opens you up to self-love; burgundy gives you a sense of being stable and centred; orange is a social colour and blue improves our intuition, while green creates a balance between us and others. Make sure you energise yourself with the colours you choose to wear, both at work and at home.

Have a **great hair** day. Looking after your locks is a great way to feel happy about yourself. Just like clothing, our hair is a means of personal expression. If our hair is a positive expression of ourselves it is likely that we are going to be happier people. Be sure to shampoo and condition your hair as much as needed, and use products that are tailored to your hair type. Use hair masques every so often for a treat, and even colour and cut your hair for a new style to show a distinctly positive you.

- ➤

Clear out your wardrobe and host a **clothing swap** with your friends. Be ruthless with your clothing and only keep the items that really fit you well and make you feel good. Even though saying goodbye to clothes can feel sad, afterwards your wardrobe will feel tidy and fresh, and the clothes that you no longer want can be offered to friends. Dress up in each other's clothes and add new pieces to your collection with your friends' help and advice. Take leftover clothes to clothes banks or charity shops, and give yourself the extra boost of knowing they have gone to a good cause.

> The happiness of life
> is made up of the little
> charities of a kiss or
> a smile, a kind look, a
> heartfelt compliment.

Samuel Taylor Coleridge

Treasure **compliments**. Learn to really listen to praise because receiving a truly meaningful compliment can greatly enhance the way we feel. Next time someone admires you, don't brush it off modestly, but thank them for it. By saying thank you we are acknowledging to them and to ourselves that we have taken on their opinions. Make a point too of saving complimentary cards and messages, so that at a later date you can re-read them and feel the boost of praise all over again.

Go out and give yourself the pleasure of buying **new perfume** or aftershave. Part of the way we look and feel can be much to do with how we smell, and what we associate those scents with. Choose a scent that suits who you are; you might prefer lighter floral scents or deeper, muskier scents. Try scenting clothing too for a longer lasting effect; when we smell great, we feel great too.

- - - - - - - - -

Give yourself a boost through **happy body posture**. Our muscles are directly connected to our brains, so the way we hold ourselves is linked to the way we are feeling. Changing your posture can change your emotions for the better; studies have found that even sitting up straight can put a more positive spin on our thoughts. Embodied cognition is the idea that our mind influences the way our bodies react, and the way we form our bodies influences our brain. So with this in mind, straighten your posture, and enjoy the benefit of more positive thoughts as a result.

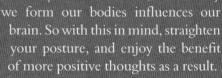

Sing **praises** into a friend or family member's voicemail. However crazy this sounds, it will make them smile or laugh, and it will certainly boost their day! Happiness can often come from giving, rather than receiving, and this doesn't necessarily mean giving someone an object. Giving someone a few moments of your time to sincerely appreciate them, or to give them some thoughtful advice, can help them feel truly treasured and strengthen your bond with them. You will not only be making a difference to their day, but to your own as well.

Often it is easier to stick within our comfort zones and concern ourselves with the things that please us, especially when we are thinking of improving *our* state of mind to become happier people. Sharing happiness with other people is a sure way to connect ourselves with others, and in turn this improves our happiness and well-being.

Dress up in your best outfit and go with a loved one for a fish 'n' chip dinner by the water. This will give you both a date to get excited about, but it won't be weighted down with pressures of expensive dining, formality and scheduled timing. Give the occasion freedom and know that you can dress up whenever you wish; you get to decide when an outing is special, and you don't have to follow anyone else's conventions!

- ➤

Always use your **best crockery**. Every day is a special day. Appreciate meal times by always using your most beautiful plates and cutlery. Often the thought of saving objects for special occasions can mean that they are rarely used and this can say rather a lot about how we value events. By using our best items every day, we are showing ourselves and the world that every moment is worth treasuring and enjoying to the full.

The mind is its own place, and in itself can make a heaven of hell, a hell of heaven.

John Milton

When it rains, pull on your **wellingtons**, run outside and jump in the biggest puddle that you can see – even the wettest weather is worth celebrating, and there's no better way to do it. The weather can be unpredictable, even in the height of summer, so try to make the most of rainy days when they appear. Finding silver linings in the things that would usually make us sad is a wonderful, constructive way to enhance our happiness levels.

– – – – – – – – – –

Release yourself from the confines of what you should be doing or what you shouldn't have done. Decide to **seize the day** and commit to doing one thing a day that makes it your own. Choose to do something that is definitively you – wear a giant sun hat on your lunch break or make a phone call for a whole hour to someone you love. The past has passed and the future is unknown, so make the most of now, and all its infinite possibilities.

Celebrate your achievements and those of your friends, with champagne more often. It is important that we recognise and celebrate even our smaller achievements, such as ticking off a goal at work, learning something new, or even carrying out some of the suggestions in this book.

When we actively celebrate an event, whether it's big or small, we are consciously recognising that we have accomplished something. Rewarding ourselves with a special event, even if it's just sitting in the garden on a summer's evening with a friend, some nibbles and a glass of bubbly, makes the achievement seem more concrete, and may even encourage us to try to achieve new things on a regular basis.

Commemorating achievements in this way also helps us to appreciate the smaller things that we do, which we often underestimate or overlook. If we ignore or diminish the things that we achieve, we may sense a feeling of disappointment in ourselves and what we do. By appreciating what we do, we begin to think more highly of ourselves, and also develop our sense of gratitude for the people who help us achieve our goals every day.

When you are upset, take a step back and ask yourself what it is that you are truly upset about. When you feel things are completely hopeless, ask yourself truly and honestly what it is that's making you feel this way. Then ask yourself if it is a problem – or if you can do anything to change it. If the answer is no, let your bad mood float away; you have nothing to be worried about, and the best thing you can do is let go and move on. If the answer is yes, think of a way to solve it. Face the issue head on and try your very best to sort it out.

- ➤

Get yourself a lucky charm to believe in. Research has shown that a lucky charm can help us to perform better. Putting our faith in something that we believe will bring us luck, takes some of the stress of a situation away and makes us feel confident and happy to take on the challenge, whether it's a test, an interview or some other tricky task. So get yourself a lucky jacket, a good luck watch or necklace, or even just cross your fingers; put your worries and fears into them, and then go out and do your best, knowing your lucky charm is there to help you.

THE BEST WAY TO CHEER YOURSELF IS TO TRY TO CHEER SOMEBODY ELSE UP.

Mark Twain

Join a **dance class**. Dancing, whether it's salsa, ballroom, ballet or even hip hop, gives us a great health boost in more ways than one. Studies have shown that people who were previously stressed, anxious or depressed reaped benefits from the positivity that they gained through dancing. Not only does dancing release happy-making endorphins, as it is a form of exercise, but the fact that it is also fun can make it easier to keep going, compared to more 'sporty' forms of exercise. This in turn contributes to sustained new healthy habits.

Sign up to a local **community challenge**, such as a marathon or fun run, or even a cycle ride from one end of the country to the other. If sport isn't your thing, you could try something as ridiculous as a sausage-mashing competition. Getting involved with the people in your area can really help to make you feel part of something, giving you confidence and a great sense of belonging.

Get yourself thinking of happiness and conjure up as many words as possible that **rhyme** with or have a connection to 'happy' and 'smile'. It is important for our brains to find happy pathways to think in, to keep us in a positive mindset. Coming up with words that relate to or rhyme with already optimistic ones, can be a good exercise to begin to train yourself to think along these channels of happiness.

Negativity is often an easy route, and can even be a hard habit to break. So whenever you feel negative thoughts sneaking into your consciousness, change your thought patterns to positive ones.

Go **beachcombing**. Visiting the beach gives us plenty to feel happy about: the sand between our toes, the sound of the lapping waves, the smell of the salty seaside air. Combing the seaside for treasure gives us a meaningful task and the possibility of finding treasures, from sea-aged pieces of wood to uniquely shaped pebbles and other unusual discoveries. Ultraviolet in the sunlight can help to improve your sense of physical and emotional well-being by stimulating the production of vitamin D. The crashing bass of the waves dispels stress and the sounds have been proven to alter waves in the brain, making you blissfully calm.

- ➤

Make time each week to **call your relatives**. Keeping in touch with members of your family is so important, especially if they live faraway. Even if the call lasts just a few minutes, catching up with family is great for raising happiness levels. Your family keep you connected with who you are and where your roots lie; they help to keep you grounded and are some of your closest friends. By making the effort to stay in touch, you will feel more content.

> IT IS ONLY POSSIBLE TO LIVE
> HAPPILY EVER AFTER ON A
> DAY TO DAY BASIS.
>
> Margaret Bonanno

Sometimes it is important to spoil ourselves with things that are a complete and utter indulgence; so find yourself a helping of the most amazing **ice-cream** and eat it in the bathtub. Running a hot bath and eating a delicious tub of ice-cream is an amazing sensation, and allowing ourselves treats like this helps to keep our positivity levels high. Of course eating healthily and exercising regularly is important too, but in every life we need a little balance, and treats are a vital part of this!

On Mother's Day, give your **Mum** a handmade card that tells her how much she means to you; the more PVA glue and glitter the better. However old you are, it is important to appreciate your mother, and what better way to do it than to put your creative efforts into a handmade card. Buying a card for the occasion is a lovely thought, but making one is even better. You can be proud of your artistic achievements – however abstract they might be – and your Mum will be touched.

On **Pancake Day** get all of your friends together and host your very own pancake Olympics in the garden. Set yourselves flipping tasks and give prizes to those with the pancakes that stay most intact. Spending time with our nearest and dearest is one of the best ways to boost how we feel, and making time to have parties and events creates room for happy memories.

Go through all of your **photo albums** and find as many hilarious and ridiculous photos as possible, then invite friends and family round for drinks, nibbles and a slideshow of everyone's 'greatest hits'.

Reminiscing is something we all love to do; it sparks conversation and laughter and it can be a great way to get to know each other – it's a great basis for making yet more memories. This is a happy event, and as you celebrate everyone's best photo moments, the room will be full of positive energy. Making time to bring together friends and family can boost our confidence, make us more social and give us joyful events to look forward to and remember for a long time.

Have a party on **Valentine's Day** for all of your single friends. Take time to send out handmade invites and spend the evening playing Cupid! For anyone who happens to be single on Valentine's Day it can be an occasion shadowed by negativity. But with your help, everyone will be able to look at it in a different light; spirits will be raised, and perhaps some of your guests might even meet the man or woman of their dreams – and who knows, you might too!

Lie on your back in the garden, the park or on the beach and **watch the clouds** as they change shape in the passing winds. Feel the warm ground beneath you and rest your eyes upon one cloud in particular. Follow it as it crosses the sky and transforms in shape. Let the bright sky absorb your stresses, and think of the ever-changing cloud shapes as representing the changes in life; they may change but it doesn't diminish their identity or their purpose.

Too much of
a good thing can
be wonderful.

Mae West

If you struggle making decisions, time yourself in the **supermarket** and make your shopping trip like a game show. Make your time spent food shopping a little more interesting, by setting yourself the task of getting everything you need within a time limit – give yourself half an hour, it's ample time to get the things you really need. Racing round the aisles eliminates the risk of spending too much time getting stressed, and gets you in the routine of having to know exactly what you need.

- - - - - - - -

Surprise a loved one with a **special supper** cooked by you, do it even if it's spaghetti alphabet on toast – just make sure you spell their name out with the letters. In this case it really is the thought that counts, and by giving someone you love a thoughtful surprise, you will bring delight to both of you. So light some candles, put on some starry-eyed music and get cooking.

Ask yourself if you enjoy what you do. We spend most of our time at work, and one of the things that can make us feel unhappy is staying in a career that brings no joy with it. We all have particular times of stress in our work, and it's normal to go through patches of boredom in what we are doing; however, if our jobs are bringing us more negativity than positivity, then there needs to be a change.

It is not always possible to get into something that feels like fun all of the time, but we can all get close to it. We need to decide for ourselves what kind of change would make us feel happiest. It could be having more fun and making more time for yourself outside work, moving to a new company or completely changing career. Life is far too short to spend your time doing something you dislike.

Aim to find **balance** between your work life and home life; being able to switch cleanly from one to the other helps to make us more stable and increases our overall happiness levels. When at work, try to focus on the task at hand, rather than wandering off into thoughts outside of work; leave that for the end of the day, there's plenty of time. Don't let your worries from work follow you around afterwards either; you can leave them in the office and pick them up again tomorrow, with the energy of a new day.

---▶

Be **prepared** for your working day. Many of us will experience stressful points at work, but preparing thoroughly for the day ahead will help to focus our thoughts and reduce stress levels. Make a packed lunch the night before and prepare what you are going to wear before you go to sleep. Make sure that you are aware of transport times and if there are likely to be any delays. Doing these things will make sure that we can get the most out of our day, and let us tackle the day's challenges calmly.

The things you need
for happiness aren't
the things you
think you need.

Irene Mueni

Failure does not exist. Spending time analysing our failures is a sure-fire route to sadness, so we need to realise that there really is no such thing as failure. Life can throw us unexpected obstacles that can stop us from achieving even the most relevant and realistic goals. So when we don't finish something or we don't manage to get something done in the way or time we expected, we can simply take a moment to learn from the experience and try again – the only way is up.

Your **imagination** is a powerful tool. Our brain and body cannot tell the difference between something we wildly imagine and something that is real, and we can use this to our advantage. If you are feeling particularly apprehensive about something, such as a job interview or a nerve-wracking speech, visualise yourself doing it and succeeding at it. Vividly imagine the people around you and feel their positive reactions to what you are doing and saying – make it seem as real as possible. Let yourself feel excited about the successful outcome.

Keep on top of your **finances**. Financial worry is one of the biggest stressors in our lives today, and it can make us feel pressured and unhappy. Taking control of what you spend and save will help you to feel happier.

Begin by having a clear-out of direct debits that you do not need. Perhaps they are online subscriptions that you no longer use; if so, get rid of them, as this will be a simple way to keep your bank balance afloat – even if it's only a small amount it makes a big difference.

If you have debts to deal with, make sure that you are paying off regular amounts on the ones with the biggest interest rates, to save as much money over time as possible. Ask yourself if the spending you do on your credit cards is essential; now could be the time to make a change and concentrate on paying off credit-card bills without running up more debt. Strive to put money away for the things that make you happiest and try your best to steer clear of debt, for a happier future.

Organise a **themed film night**. You could play films you used to enjoy as a child or even a selection of the all-time soppiest rom-coms. Whatever you choose, invite all of your friends, make popcorn and have fun watching some of your favourite films with them. Spending time with your friends is a great way to boost your happiness – and theirs – and there's nothing like laughing and crying your way through films with them.

Book a **plane ticket** to see a friend who lives far away. If one of your friends moves away it can be easy to lose touch with them, but by making a special effort to see them, you can bring back the magic to your relationship. We all need a break from the day-to-day, so bite the bullet and book a ticket to go out to them. Your positivity will be well rewarded, and with luck you'll get a return visit before too long.

> Do what you have always done and you'll get what you have always got.

Sue Knight

Start a **conga line** while waiting for a bus! Sprinkle fun throughout your day, no matter how ordinary a situation usually can be. Turning things like waiting for the bus into something fun can really brighten our moods, and the moods of others too. Let go of your inhibitions more than you usually do, and know that you are able to take control of situations; by sharing fun with other people, you bring more happiness to their lives, as well as your own.

Write a **love letter** to the object of your desire and post it… signing it is optional. Releasing our fears and expressing our true feelings can be liberating, and taking a risk to share our feelings with others can bring us great happiness. Remember to express yourself with kindness and sensitivity, and consider the feelings of the object of your affection. It's easy to worry too much about the various pitfalls that may never happen, so just jump in head-first and see what happens. It could be something great.

Search your **social media** sites for friends you have lost touch with over the years and send them all lovely messages. Perhaps you could even organise a reunion or meet-up with everyone. Life carries us apart on strong tides and we often realise, only quite slowly, that we have lost touch with great friends. All it takes is a simple message to be reunited again.

Where are you most positive? Identifying where and in what aspects of your life you are **happiest**, is a useful exercise in recognising the happiest parts of you and what you do; it also highlights the bits that you really need to work on and what you need to do to be a more contented person.

You could be at your happiest being a parent, but perhaps parenting young children is coming to an end and it is now time to get back into work. Work may be something that makes you feel unhappy, or it may have done so in the past. One key point about happiness is change; changing a situation is the only way to improve it, so identify and face the problems in life that bring your mood down, no matter how big or small, and make a positive change. Try a new job, and choose that career path by using the situations that make you most happy; it could be taking care of other people's young children or it could even be used as a chance to get back into something you really love. Be happier by knowing your happy strengths and let those radiate into other aspects of life.

Write down your worries. Periods of worry are unavoidable in life, but we have the power to choose how we deal with them, and the simple fact of realising this can be a great help in itself. Whether your worries involve finances, friends, family members, work, health or something else, if you give yourself the time to write down the things that are bothering you, you'll gain a fresh perspective on the situation. As a result, your mind will feel clearer and you'll be more prepared to deal with whatever is troubling you.

- ➤

Try **progressive relaxation**. This technique sounds incredibly simple, but it is a very effective way of releasing tension and anxiety, and can be a great aid in helping you sleep better. In a relaxed position, start by clenching your toes together tightly, and then release, feeling the physical effect of relaxation. You might like to try telling yourself, 'I am relaxing my feet, they are now relaxed.' Work your way up your body, tensing and relaxing each muscle group. By the time you reach the top of your head, you will be totally relaxed.

SURROUND YOURSELF WITH ONLY PEOPLE WHO ARE GOING TO LIFT YOU UP HIGHER.

Oprah Winfrey

Be a **tourist** in your own town or city. While racing to get to work every day, many of us forget to really appreciate where we live: the buildings and landmarks, the distant hills and the many shops in the foreground. For one day, become a tourist and observe and appreciate the place you call home. Even if you think you have seen all of the famous buildings, you may not have looked at them very closely. Take an open-top bus ride or a guided tour, visit museums and read all of the leaflets on the way. You may be surprised at how much you learn!

- - - - - - - - -

Make your **dream house** out of Lego. Even if the vision for your perfect home is ludicrously extravagant: swimming pools, decadent shrubbery, wraparound verandas and whole walls of glass, put it together with Lego and place it somewhere in your home where you will see it every day. Silly as it may seem, making our dreams into something concrete – however small – can be just the motivation we need to turn them into realities one day.

Write that book. Most of us have daydreamed about being a writer, and we all have something to share with the world, whether it's a humorous autobiography, a spine-chilling thriller, a story that will enthral children, or something completely different. Well, no matter how daunting it may seem, take on the challenge and write a book.

The wonderful thing about writing your own book is that you are in complete control. You may choose to set yourself deadlines, so you have regular goals to aim for, or you might prefer to write in short bursts whenever the mood takes you. This is your project and you can do it however you want to. The most important thing is to do it.

As well as unleashing creativity, writing can be a great form of therapy. Seeing our thoughts on paper or on screen can give us new insights, and sometimes we find it easier to be more honest when we know that we are writing just for ourselves.

Anxiety is the
dizziness of
freedom.

Søren Kierkegaard

Learn the **dance moves** from your favourite part of *Dirty Dancing* and stun your friends on the dance floor as you rock out to '(I've Had) The Time of My Life'. Dancing is good for the mood as well as for our physical fitness, and recreating classic dance moments like this is guaranteed to make you and your partner smile.

Spend a day doing all your normal activities in your normal way, but without wearing any underwear. Make sure your new look doesn't reveal too much, as you don't want to cause public disorder, and then step out into the street revelling in your new-found freedom. Doing something a little **mischievous** can be thrilling and really quite fun, and this small subversive gesture is bound to keep you smiling all day.

Create a **time capsule** with photographs, mementos and secrets inside. Bury it in the garden with the strict instruction that it cannot be opened or unearthed for at least 10 years.

Putting together a capsule of memories will not only give you fond memories in 10 years' time, but the process of putting the box together gives you the opportunity to relive happy moments and 'curate' a collection of all the things that are meaningful to you. Ask each member of your family to add something that's significant to them, and combine this with newspaper cuttings, film ticket stubs, stamps and a handwritten letter or card to your future self, so that when you finally open it a decade from now, you will receive the gift – from yourself – of a detailed picture of your life right now.

While you walk around today, smile at everyone that passes you; you'll be amazed at how many people smile back. Smiles are contagious and scientists say that even chocolate cannot match the stimulation the brain gets from a simple smile. When we feel joy our brains tell us to grin, and when we grin it reinforces that joyful feeling. Smiling can help to reduce the stress we feel in mind and body, much like the effect of sleeping. So smile and enjoy knowing that you are spreading your joy far and wide.

Go roller-skating. Equip yourself with boots and kneepads, take yourself to the nearest park and let the rolling adventure begin! Do it with friends and have fun racing each other and trying new manoeuvres. Not only will you enjoy the exercise, but you'll also feel the benefit of sunshine and fresh air on your skin. Trying something new and a little daring will make you feel at your best.

A GROUP OF YOUNG MALE DEER TRAVELLING TOGETHER MAY HAVE DIFFERENT LENGTHS OF ANTLERS, BUT THEY WILL LEAVE THE SAME HOOF-PRINTS.

Bhutanese proverb

Stargaze and wonder at the immensity of the universe. Instead of hurrying indoors at night, take the time to look above you at the night sky, gazing into the darkness between each glittering point of light. Learn to identify constellations such as Orion, Leo and the Great Bear, and study the ancient cratered surface of the moon, so familiar yet so very far away. Allow yourself to marvel at the fact that you exist as part of the vast landscape of the universe, and feel a sense of awe as you realise that you have the power to make the world better, however small you are in the grand scheme of things.

Get on your bike and **cycle**, whether it's from Land's End to John o'Groats or simply to the other end of town. Cycling is great exercise, and knowing that we are travelling lightly on the earth will make us feel happier, as well as healthier. Taking the time to cycle or walk journeys that we often take by car, gives us the opportunity to experience our surroundings more deeply, and also provides a sense of achievement when we arrive, glowing and full of energy.

- - - - - - - -

Grind your own **coffee beans** and try adding a few extra ingredients to your daily brew. You could try a dash of chocolate powder, a pinch of cinnamon, a vanilla pod or a handful of hazelnuts. Give your new blend an exotic name and let all your friends try it; you could even take it to work and share it with your colleagues. Creating new flavours is exciting and brings a little boost of joy to an everyday activity.

Learn to **surf** at your nearest beach, and feel the thrill of riding the waves. Believe it or not, our brains thrive on challenges, and learning new skills has a positive effect on our well-being. Throughout our lives our brains are capable of learning many great things and by constantly being open to new endeavours, we stay curious and engaged with the world. Learning to surf is a great way to achieve a sense of accomplishment, self-confidence and resilience, which will benefit you in other areas of your life.

Eastern wisdom has taught for a long time that happiness is a skill that can be learned, and research has told us that happiness can be enhanced through training, thanks to the neuroplasticity of our brains. Stimulating ourselves with new and challenging interests can be a great way to train our brains to be happier. Get down to the beach and get learning. You never know: surfing could be your next great love.

Write **philosophical quotes** that mean a lot to you on slips of paper, and leave them where friends, colleagues or even strangers may find them. Learning from the wisdom of others is wonderful, but spreading that wisdom further is even better. You could even post your favourite quotes on social media, for thousands of people to learn from.

Treat yourself well. It's all too easy to forget to assess our own performance and character with the love and care that we automatically show to others, thanks to the stresses of work and other daily routines. Think of your best friends and imagine the way that you treat them – you deserve the kind thoughts you give to them just as much as they do. Give yourself a break, slow down and realise that you are a valuable person too, worthy of love and respect.

One joy
scatters a
hundred griefs.

Chinese proverb

Plan a **holiday** to a destination in your home country. Many of us have travelled more intensively in faraway countries, seeing exotic sights such as the souks of Morocco or the beaches of Jamaica, than we have in the countries where we live. It is worth reminding ourselves that booking time away to explore nearby territories, can be just as interesting as visiting distant lands.

- - - - - - - -

Throw yourself into a new **creative venture**. It could be anything at all, from taking up crochet or starting a patchwork quilt, to building a shed in your garden or painting a mural on the side of your house. The key is to find something that you're passionate about; if it feels a little daunting, so much the better! The new project will give you something fun to think about and plan for, and you will have a proud sense of achievement when you've finished. By then, you'll be raring to go on your **next** project…

Start a **blog** and write regular pieces for it. Writing is a great way to get down our emotions, and in modern times, what better way to write than on a blog that is out there for the world to see. Be creative and take your own artistic photographs to go with it – treat it like your personal magazine. You can even add videos – the sky is the limit!

There are thousands of interesting blogs already on the internet, so if you need some inspiration, have a hunt around until you find the topics and writing styles that really speak to you. You could write about all your diverse interests and experiences, or focus on a single topic that's important to you: this is your blog and you can do what you like with it.

As blogs have a global audience, you may be surprised just how far your words can reach. The feedback you receive from readers can be a great confidence booster, but remember: the most important thing is that you express what matters to you. You never know how much your words could encourage or inspire the people who read them.

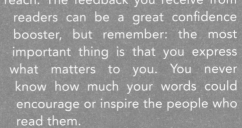

Spring-clean the **desktop** of your computer or tablet and get rid of all those superfluous files, old emails and programs you no longer need. Choose a special photo for your background wallpaper, so you feel cheered and inspired whenever you close down your programs. You'll find that the benefits of this virtual clean-up are just as powerful as the benefits of decluttering the files and folders on your real desktop.

Take your seat on a **boat or ferry**, and enjoy experiencing life on the water. You could travel to a nearby island, and spend the day exploring all its sights, or you could take a river tour and enjoy watching the scenery pass by. However long or short your journey, you will see familiar surroundings from a new angle, and as your boat floats away from the shore, you can leave your worries on land and enjoy your new-found sense of exploration and freedom.

IF YOU WANT OTHERS TO BE HAPPY,

PRACTISE COMPASSION.

IF YOU WANT TO BE HAPPY,

PRACTISE COMPASSION.

Dalai Lama

Buy a **waterproof camera** – a cheap one is fine – and head out to the beach to take some underwater photos. We very rarely get a chance to see what's going on under the waves, but with your new camera in hand you'll be able to capture images that are both beautiful and memorable. Whether you photograph swaying seaweed or colourful shoals of fish, you'll enjoy seeing and sharing images of a world we don't often see.

- - - - - - - -

Go to your **favourite city** and allow yourself to get completely and utterly lost. You could be down in the narrow promenades of Venice amongst swathes of busy tourists, or you could be wandering through London and decide to have some tea while you watch the world go by. Moving through a city without a firm destination lets you see sights with fresh eyes, and you never know what you might discover on your travels.

Learn to make **sushi**. A Japanese delicacy, sushi is prepared with fresh fish, vegetables and rice, often wrapped in a savoury layer of seaweed.

Scientists believe that sushi is one of the reasons that the Japanese are amongst the healthiest people in the world. Its staple ingredients are packed with goodness: fish contains omega-3, which is linked to heart protection and improved circulation and seaweed is rich in concentrated minerals, including iodine, calcium, iron and magnesium. Even the wasabi that adds heat to each mouthful is good for you, as it has been found to be beneficial to the teeth.

Although it requires patience and practice to make a neat sushi roll, it is great fun to experiment with this cuisine, and the fact that it is good for you adds to its happiness-inducing qualities.

Once you've learned how to make some sushi dishes, invite your friends round for a sushi party. Place all the items on plates in the centre of the table, so everyone can help themselves and experience the same flavours. It's fun to use chopsticks, but nobody will mind if you opt for knives and forks instead. For an even deeper shared experience, invite your friends over earlier to help prepare the feast.

Organise a celebration. Discover special occasions that you never knew about, and mark them in style. For example, you could celebrate International Chocolate Day on 13 September with a chocolate fondue party, and International Day of Happiness on 20 March with a back-to-back screening of your favourite funny movies. With just a little research, you'll discover that there is something special to celebrate on every day of the year.

IF YOU'VE GOT NOTHING
TO DANCE ABOUT, FIND A
REASON TO SING.

Melody Carstairs

Go **UFO** spotting. Wander under the stars with your friends and look up into the sky together, to see if you can spot any extra-terrestrial activity. Although it's often tempting to stay indoors in the warm, walking through the quiet night together will give you all a refreshing new experience. Even if you don't spot any alien spacecraft, you may spot nocturnal animals going about their business, or even a shooting star crossing the heavens.

Try a new type of **fruit**. Getting through our five a day can sometimes feel like an uphill struggle, but being more adventurous with the fruit we eat can help us to consume more of it. Aim for a rainbow of fruits for maximum health benefits. Whether you prefer treats found at the supermarket, such as passion fruit and mango, or the more unusual delights in your local specialist shops, bringing a little extra variety into your fruit bowl will be good for your health and your happiness levels.

– – – – – – – – –

On a sunny day, go outside, sit somewhere comfortable on the grass, and make a beautiful **daisy chain**. You can revisit this simple childhood pleasure by yourself, but it's even more fun to do this with a friend and see who can make the longest chain. Reminding ourselves of childhood games is a great way to keep our inner child happy and entertained, and makes a lovely change from pretending to be serious grown-ups the rest of the time.

Zip it. For an entire day try to be aware of what you say, and if the words you are about to utter are negative, see if you can get by without saying them at all. It's very easy for negativity to saturate our conversations, in the form of complaints and criticisms, but life can be much more pleasant if we choose to focus on the positives instead.

When we vocalise negative opinions and emotions, these are what our minds – and those of our listeners – focus on. Making this into a habit can lead to negative thinking patterns, and although we may think we're just letting off steam, sometimes we are in fact just making ourselves more unhappy.

Make a change and aim, for just one day, to avoid all negative and downhearted statements. This doesn't mean that we should aim to say positive things just for the sake of it, however; we may choose to say nothing at all, and if a bad situation arises we can come up with solutions and suggestions for ways around the obstacles.

Appreciate the changing **seasons**, particularly as the year draws to a close and summer's heat fades away. Wake up early on an autumn morning and watch the dew sparkling in sunlight on yesterday's cobwebs. Observe carefully as the days grow shorter, and the trees clothe themselves in glowing red and golden robes. Enjoy wrapping yourself in long scarves and light coats, and allow yourself to be charmed by the rays of the Indian summer sunshine.

Go down to the **harbour** and imagine all the journeys you could take, whether on a fishing vessel or a container ship, to shores both near and far. Goods reach our shores from places we will never visit, and products leave from our factories and farms to go to customers we'll never meet. Enjoy envisioning distant lands and the people who live in them. And who knows – one day you might stand in a foreign harbour, looking at ships on their way back to this very spot.

When the mind is pure, joy follows like a shadow that never leaves.

Buddha

Play **word association games** with your friends and get fascinating new insights into how each other's minds work. These games are great for understanding the subconscious and can also help us to think laterally, finding new solutions to problems from our day-to-day lives.

- - - - - - - - -

Make **bunting** and hang it up in a place where you will see it every day; it could be your bedroom, the kitchen, the bathroom, even your office. Making bunting can be a simple sewing project for using up scrap bits of material that you may have around the house; it is also a great way to bring decoration and a feeling of fun into your rooms. When the weather is mild, you can also display your bunting draped in trees and shrubbery in the garden – it's a perfect background for outdoor celebrations.

Learn to make the perfect **cappuccino** and invite a close friend round to share a cup of frothy, coffee perfection with you. Bake biscotti too, if you have time, and your home will smell delicious and welcoming when your friend arrives.

Thoughtful gifts are a great way to show people that we love and appreciate them, gifts involving food and drink are always gladly received.

Coffee making is an art, and once mastered, can be very rewarding. Here are a few handy tips for making really great coffee: use fresh coffee, rather than the instant variety; if you don't have a coffee grinder, consider asking a local shop to grind some beans freshly for you; and for a really good taste, use bottled spring water instead of water from the tap.

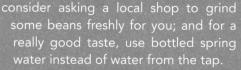

People-watch in your local high street, and make up ludicrous backstories for the people that catch your eye. Taking time to sit, relax and observe the world going by is a great antidote to the stresses and strains that assail us during our daily lives. Engaging your imagination as you indulge in a spot of people-watching is a wonderful – and slightly subversive – therapy that's sure to have you feeling calmer and happier in no time.

Revisit a **childhood holiday destination**. Although we cannot literally travel back in time to relive happy memories, going back to places that are close to our hearts can be very rewarding. Perhaps you had a favourite location for family camping trips, or a memorable ski trip to the mountains. Revisiting places where we've been happy before, is a wonderful way to revive forgotten memories and create new happy moments to remember.

THERE ARE ALWAYS FLOWERS

FOR THOSE WHO

WANT TO SEE THEM.

Henri Matisse

Take part in a **dog-walking scheme**, and enjoy strolling through the streets and playing in the park with other people's pets. We are innately social beings, and scientists have found that spending time with animals can greatly improve our well-being and happiness. With their unquestioning loyalty and sense of play, pets improve our sense of belonging and self-esteem.

- - - - - - - -

Have a treat and **toast marshmallows** over a campfire. For a healthier twist on this tradition, you could also try toasting strawberries, dates or chunks of banana. Spending time outdoors with friends, sharing delicious fire-roasted treats and talking long into the evening, is a perfect recipe for a happiness boost.

Get ready for an adventure and sign yourself up for the **Mongol Rally**. There's no fixed route, just a start point and an end point, and the rest is up to you, as you find your way across 10,000 miles of snow-peaked mountains and sandy deserts.

All you need is a tiny budget car, and a fund of £1,000 that you have raised for charity. In return you will have absolutely no back-up, no support and no set route, so it is completely up to you and your friends to plot your own path. The Mongol Rally embraces the idea of being utterly lost, and it will test your mechanical, navigational, language and social skills, pushing you perhaps further than you've ever been pushed before. The adventure allows you to see parts of the world you may never have encountered, and it is likely that it will change your way of viewing the world. It's not without risks – in fact it's full of them – but along the way you're certain to make plenty of new friends and travel through places most people will never see, and that is sure to bring a smile to your face.

Go for a Turkish bath. Otherwise known as a *hammam*, a Turkish bath is a relaxing activity that is traditional in both Turkey and Morocco; it's a perfect way for tired travellers to detox and cleanse. There are usually three separate chambers, the first being a hot steam room, the next a warm room to scrub and a cooler one to relax in. *Hammams* can also offer services such as aromatherapy, reflexology, facial masks and Indian head massages. Relax, cleanse and be happy.

Go somewhere with a broad, uncluttered horizon and gaze at it. The less detail there is to concentrate on in the foreground, the further you can sink into reverie. Looking out towards the horizon gives us a sense of the world's sheer magnitude. Losing ourselves in thought as we stare into the distance can be a great way to come up with creative new ideas, and at the very least it will be a valuable opportunity for you to reflect and relax.

The soul's joy
lies in doing.

Percy Bysshe Shelley

Take a friend out for a **surprise lunch date**. We all need a break from eating sandwiches at our desks, and going somewhere a little fancy – or very fancy, if it's a special occasion – is sure to cheer you both up for the rest of the day. As you chat together over delicious food and drink, the cares of the day will seem far away, and you'll both return to work refreshed and ready for action.

Learn some **origami** techniques. An ancient Japanese legend says that if you fold one thousand crane birds with paper, a wish of your choice will come true. In truth, the act of folding so many birds is likely to steer you down meditative pathways of reflection that lead you to solve your own problems and come to terms with whatever is troubling you. There are many books and websites to show you how to start, and an infinite number of shapes you can create.

- - - - - - - - -

Find a **pond or stream** and lose yourself in thought watching dragonflies, water boatmen, fish and frogs; it is nature's answer to meditation. Even if you live in a crowded town or city, a pond can be just as inspiring as a wild lake in the countryside. Let the gentle movement of the water soothe you and lead you to a peaceful sense of calm joy.

Start a **dinner club** with friends and create a reason for you all to come together and enjoy each other's company. Often, as you get older your commitments increase and your time becomes more precious. By setting up a fixed date – perhaps the last Friday of every month – to meet, you create some space in your schedule to dedicate to friends. There are many ways you could set up a dinner club; it could be that you each bring a dish to try or perhaps take turns cooking for a themed evening. Perhaps you could simply enjoy 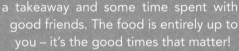 a takeaway and some time spent with good friends. The food is entirely up to you – it's the good times that matter!

The next time you find yourself about to use a lift, take the stairs. The lift might seem the most appealing option but if you take the stairs, you're giving yourself a mini workout, and over time, these workouts will really boost your fitness. With a little time and persistence, you'll soon be striding effortlessly to the very top, and your heart will thank you for it.

Watch a film you used to love as a child. Although your daily life is packed with adult responsibilities, you'll find yourself quickly slipping back into the wholehearted reactions of a child as you watch it. Nothing is quite as funny as something that made you laugh when you were a child. So take a trip down memory lane and let yourself be a child again!

An unshared
happiness is
not happiness.

Boris Pasternak

A romance can benefit greatly from moments of silliness. Get dressed up to the nines with your partner, and have a **romantic meal for two** at a fast food restaurant. There may be a few whispers and you might feel a little silly at first, but you'll soon find that laughing at yourself develops into laughing together. Even if the food is forgettable, the memory of your special date will last forever.

- - - - - - - - -

Make **paper chains** from old magazines or any other paper you have lying around, and festoon your home with them. As well as bringing fun to your interior décor, they will also remind you that everything has a purpose: even paper that's bound for the recycling bin can become a thing of beauty. Once you've started with paper chains, you'll soon find yourself looking at other disposable, everyday objects and wondering what you can create.

If you have an area of expertise or a hobby that you are skilled in, consider **offering your services to others**. Maybe you could teach your skills to a friend or family member; alternatively, a local school or community group might welcome a talk or masterclass from someone with your knowledge.

Not only will this give you a new way to enjoy something you're passionate about, but teaching others helps reinforce your knowledge. Unexpected questions could help you look at a familiar subject in a new way and you could well be as inspired by others, as they are by you.

Make a **winter wonderland** in your home. Snow is one of nature's wonders and for many it occurs too rarely. Instead of wishing and hoping for snow, take matters into your own hands, by draping white sheets over furniture, hanging up snowflake decorations and bringing your old, cuddly polar bear down from the attic. Invite your friends round for mulled wine, and enjoy a taste of winter, at any time of the year!

◀ –

Alternatively, transform your house into a summer **beach scene**. You don't have to pour sand everywhere: a generous use of beach towels, deck chairs and inflatable flamingos will be just as effective. Put on some summery tunes, make a pitcher or two of sangria, and enjoy the ultimate indoor beach holiday with your friends.

The greatest
healing therapy is
friendship and love.

Hubert Humphrey

Dancing is a fantastic form of exercise, and strutting your stuff energetically can release the same endorphins as a work-out, as well as being good for your whole body. Hitting the dance floor also gives you a chance to express yourself. You don't have to be an expert; just move to the music in any way you choose, and feel your happiness levels rise with each new song.

Carry out an **archaeological dig** in your own back garden, making sure to avoid any pet graveyards. You may only get to know your local worms and creepy crawlies, but it is entirely possible that you will find something of note. Items that were rubbish only a decade or two ago can be sources of nostalgia – a can of long-discontinued drink, or a coin from years ago can set you on a journey of discovery.

Start small. Setting out to achieve your dreams is a fantastic endeavour but can seem a little daunting to start. You may not be ready for a major change, such as quitting your job or moving abroad, just yet – most of us aren't! – but if you put in some thought and planning, you will find lots of small steps you can take to make those bigger dreams come true. If your dream is to own your own café, perhaps sign up to a night class in cookery or business. If you would like to travel or live abroad, download an app to help you learn the language of your desired destination. Taking baby steps towards your dream will help you feel productive, and will inspire you to keep going until you achieve your goal.

Spend time at your local library. As well as enjoying the many resources the library can offer you, from books to DVDs and much more, you will also find community groups you can join or support, and children's reading challenges – you can join in with your own child or participate as a helper if you are child-free. Libraries are also great sources of information about what's happening in the wider community, so there's no telling where a trip to the library might take you.

- -

Start a book club. It's nice to spend time with your friends, but it's really satisfying when you have a shared endeavour, such as all reading the same book and coming together to discuss it. You can take turns to suggest books for the group to enjoy, and you are bound to find your discussions ranging far and wide; debates about plot developments or key characters can spiral out into deep conversations about our opinions, experiences and perspectives.

> PEOPLE WILL FORGET
> WHAT YOU DID, BUT PEOPLE
> WILL NEVER FORGET HOW YOU
> MADE THEM FEEL.
>
> Maya Angelou

Initiate a **brief encounter** with your partner. Arrange to meet ever so briefly, during a normal day. The tease of seeing your loved one for only a moment, exchanging a kiss or gifts, will lead you to think of them for the rest of the day and yearn for their company. This helps recreate the thrill of your first days together.

Play **board games** with friends and family members. Not only is a games session a great way to socialise, but it will also stimulate the brain. Different games offer different challenges, calling on your reasoning ability, your planning skills or your strategic techniques. Just make sure you agree on the rules beforehand, and remember to be flexible if anyone gets a little too competitive!

- - - - - - - - -

Go on a tandem **bike ride** with a friend, or if you're really brave, hire some unicycles. We all know that more exercise would be good for us, but sometimes it can feel a little bit too much like hard work. Finding a fun new activity to try is a great way to get yourself moving while keeping happiness levels high. So find a friend and some unusual wheels, and start a new adventure together!

If you ever find yourself feeling sad, give yourself permission to **accept help**, whether from a friend or a professional. You are not alone and do not have to bear your burdens by yourself. Whether you have a practical problem that needs fixing, or an emotional burden that is weighing you down, you don't need to suffer in silence. Psychologists Jecker and Landy found that people who were asked for a favour by others, liked the recipient more after doing it. Friendship is a two way street, and relying on each other can help one person feel supported and the other useful or needed. After all, if you would do it for a friend, why not let them do the same for you? It may even be that you would like to talk to a medical professional about your concerns. Give yourself permission to do so.

Add a twist to your New Year resolutions by making them part of a group challenge with your friends. Striving towards self-improvement is a valuable thing to do, but sometimes it's fun and beneficial to take on a challenge just for its own sake. To get the weirdest and most random ideas, host a party and ask each person to write down an aim or target, then drop them into a hat. Everyone draws one at random and takes that on as one of their resolutions.

Add a crafty touch to an indulgence, to turn it into an achievement as well as a pleasure. If you plan to enjoy a bowl of ice-cream, think ahead and make your own chocolate bowl to make the treat complete. Melt chocolate and when cool but still liquid, pour over a balloon. When it's dry, pop the balloon. Voila! A chocolate bowl, ready and waiting, for a scoop or three of ice-cream.

CHANGE YOUR THOUGHTS

AND YOU CHANGE THE WORLD.

Norman Vincent Peale

Construct a **rope swing** in your garden and make the most of it. You will be out amongst nature, indulging in a childish activity and feeling the wind in your hair. The little stresses of the day won't be able to get a word in, with so much fun and happiness taking up all your attention.

- - - - - - - - -

Plan a **pilgrimage**; it can be to a site of religious or secular importance, depending on your interests. Visiting places of great spiritual significance gives us a sense of our place in the world and can provide inspiration and a sense of being part of a 'bigger picture'. Ideas for secular pilgrimages include locations of historical significance, monuments or memorials or a location relevant to a person you admire.

Forgive yourself and, where necessary, forget too. If you are self-conscious, start small; let go of the time you said the wrong thing at a party or accidentally bumped into a stranger in the street. Without the power of foresight, you couldn't have avoided it! Then focus on the times you knew you were acting wrongly – have you made amends, would you act differently if doing it again, are you fully aware of your actions? If the answer to all of those questions is 'yes' then you simply cannot do any more; you will be feeling bad for feeling bad's sake. Stop punishing yourself and accept that you have learned a lesson, as all humans do. You deserve to be happy!

Many of our happiest days are often national holidays such as Christmas. These provide us with anticipation and an excuse to celebrate, eat delicious food and give and receive. Take the time to focus on what really matters about these occasions: it's not the expensive presents, it's having fun together that really counts.

There are many websites that provide information on the nature in your area, and your local library or tourist office will have leaflets, too. Learning more about our environment helps us feel more connected to the world, in an era when we're so often trapped behind screens and other gadgets. Download a nature guide and go on a hunt to see what animals and plants you can find. Even if you live in an urban area, you could be surprised at what you see when you start to really look around you.

Life is a great
big canvas, and
you should throw
all the paint
on it you can.

Danny Kaye

Christmas decorations bring a festive mood to our homes and offices – but decorations don't have to be only for Christmas! You can celebrate the changing seasons with **decorations all year round**, from boughs of spring blossoms to tropical summer images, to displays of autumn leaves – and much more. Marking our passage through the year in this way also reminds us to make the most of what each season has to offer.

- - - - - - - - - -

As well as decorating your home and work space to celebrate the best of each season, you can give your mood a lift by creating **seasonal playlists**. Make your journey to work more fun each day with songs celebrating new beginnings in the spring, holidays in the summer, achieving success in the crisp days of autumn, and snuggling up on cold and frosty winter evenings. The only limit is your imagination.

Observe the **summer and winter solstices** and the **spring and autumn equinoxes**. These four dates are astronomical events that humans have used to measure the calendar for thousands of years. The summer solstice is the longest day of the year and the winter solstice the shortest, while the spring and autumn equinoxes are the two dates of the year where day and night are of equal length. Celebrating these dates could make you feel a part of a tradition reaching back for millennia, and also helps you to be mindful about the passing year. Celebrate in the great outdoors – perhaps watching the sun rise for the winter solstice and the sun set for the summer solstice – and feel connected to something bigger than yourself.

Set aside a little time and research your **family tree**. A good place to start is to seek out the older members of your family and ask about their memories of *their* older relatives. They are a living link to the past and you are sure not only to learn helpful details, but also hear anecdotes about your loved ones' pasts that you never knew before.

Another rainy day idea is to **upcycle your old clothes**. Even if you're not an expert with a sewing machine, there are lots of other, simpler techniques you can use to add some pizazz to a garment. Try fabric paint, stencils or iron-on badges, for an easy start to clothing customisation, and let your creativity take you on a magical mystery tour.

LIFE IS THE FLOWER FOR WHICH LOVE IS THE HONEY.

Victor Hugo

Invite nature into your life by **building a rockery** in your garden. Popular garden design is often not very nature-friendly, with the open lawn and small borders providing little shelter or habitat for wild creatures. A wild flower corner can be a haven for bees and butterflies, and a rockery creates dark and sheltered spaces for insects and small creatures.

Modern life often demands that you record a moment even as you are experiencing it. If you want to switch off for the day but would still like a memento, consider **sketching** the scene instead of snapping it on your smartphone. Buy a sketchbook and some pencils and take them out for the day. When you want to capture a moment, draw it, in whatever way feels most natural for you. You'll feed your creative brain and still have something to remember the day by.

Do you remember all the adventures you used to have as a child? You hadn't learned to be self-conscious yet, and you weren't afraid to sing or play pretend and let your imagination run free. Reclaim some of that emotional freedom and **write a play** with your friends, acting it out for an audience if you wish. You'll be surprised at how nourished your emotions and creativity will be by the exercise, not to mention the fun you'll have spending time with friends.

A Happy Tomorrow

By the time you've read all these suggestions and put some of them into practice, you'll be brimming over with new ideas of how to bring more happiness into your own life, and how to spread joy to others around you, too.

Whether you prefer wild and wacky projects, or mindful moments that help you reconnect with your peaceful inner self, I hope that the tips in *Project Happiness* have encouraged and inspired you. We all deserve to be happy, and the journey of discovery and exploration is just as important as the destination! May your journey be full of fun, creativity and (of course) true happiness.

YOU ARE NEVER TOO LATE TO SET ANOTHER GOAL OR DREAM A NEW DREAM.

C. S. Lewis

If you're interested in finding out
more about our books, find us on Facebook
at Summersdale Publishers and follow
us on Twitter at @Summersdale.

www.summersdale.com